LOS ANGELES
ANGELS

STARS, STATS, HISTORY, AND MORE!

BY CONOR BUCKLEY

Published by The Child's World®
1980 Lookout Drive • Mankato, MN 56003-1705
800-599-READ • www.childsworld.com

ISBN 9781503828261
LCCN 2018944839

Printed in the United States of America
PAO2392

Photo Credits:
Cover: Joe Robbins (2).
Interior: AP Images: 9, Lennox McLendon 19; Dream-
stime.com: Ypkim 13, Ffooter 14; Newscom: David Den-
nis/Icon SMI 10, Karl Mondon/KRT 17, John Cordes/Icon
SMI 23, Brian Rothmuller/Icon Sportwire DHZ 27, V.J.
Lovero/Icon SMI 29; Joe Robbins 5, 6, 24 (2).

About the Author

Conor Buckley is a lifelong
baseball fan now studying
for a career in esports. His
books in this series are his first
published works.

On the Cover

Main photo: Superstar Mike Trout
Inset: Hall of Famer
Vladimir Guerrero

CONTENTS

GO, ANGELS!

The Los Angeles Angels have been playing in the Major Leagues since 1961. They have played at three different stadiums in Southern California. For many years the Angels were one of the worst teams in the AL West. In 2002, they finally made it to the World Series. They won! The Angels have had many talented players. Fans love to cheer for the Angels and their mascot, the Rally Monkey!

Mike Trout slugs homers and runs fast. Many fans ➤
think he is the best player in baseball today.

WHO ARE THE ANGELS?

The Los Angeles Angels play in the American League (AL). The AL is part of Major League Baseball (MLB). MLB also includes the National League (NL). There are 30 teams in MLB. The winner of the AL plays the winner of the NL in the World Series. The Angels' first and only World Series win came in 2002.

 Shortstop Andrelton Simmons was one of the AL's top hitters in 2018.

WHERE THEY CAME FROM

The Los Angeles Angels began as a **minor league** team. They played in the Pacific Coast League. The team's home was Wrigley Field in L.A. They were owned by Gene Autry, a movie and country music star. In 1961, MLB added new teams. The Angels joined the big leagues! In 1965, the team moved south of L.A. to Anaheim. Their new name became the California Angels. In 1997, they changed it to the Anaheim Angels. In 2005, they changed again, this time to the Los Angeles Angels of Anaheim! Finally, they dropped "of Anaheim" in 2016.

Ted Kluszewski finished his long big-league ➤
career in the Angels' first season, 1961.

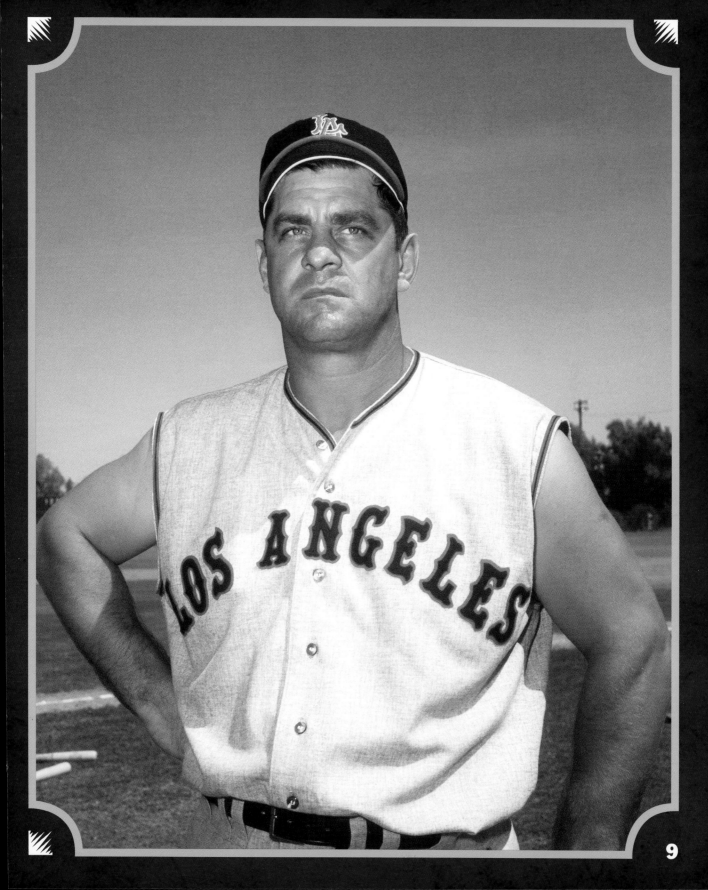

WHO THEY PLAY

The Angels play 162 games in a season. That's a lot of baseball! They play most of their games against other AL teams. The Angels are part of the AL West Division. The other AL West teams are the Houston Astros, the Oakland Athletics, the Seattle Mariners, and the Texas Rangers. AL teams sometimes play NL teams. The Angels and the NL's Los Angeles Dodgers are big **rivals**. When the two teams play, the games are called the "Freeway Series."

◄ *Angels sluggers battle great Dodgers pitchers in the Freeway Series.*

WHERE THEY PLAY

The Angels play their home games at Angel Stadium. The stadium is nicknamed "The Big A." A large A-shaped sign stands outside. The halo at the top of the Big A lights up when the Angels win. The stadium is also famous for statues of two large Angels hats. Inside each hat is a tag that reads "Size $649^{1}/_{2}$"!

Angels fans are happy when the halo on top of the "Big A" lights up. ➤

NOBODY
BEATS
HOWARD'S

ANGEL
STADIUM
OF ANAHEIM

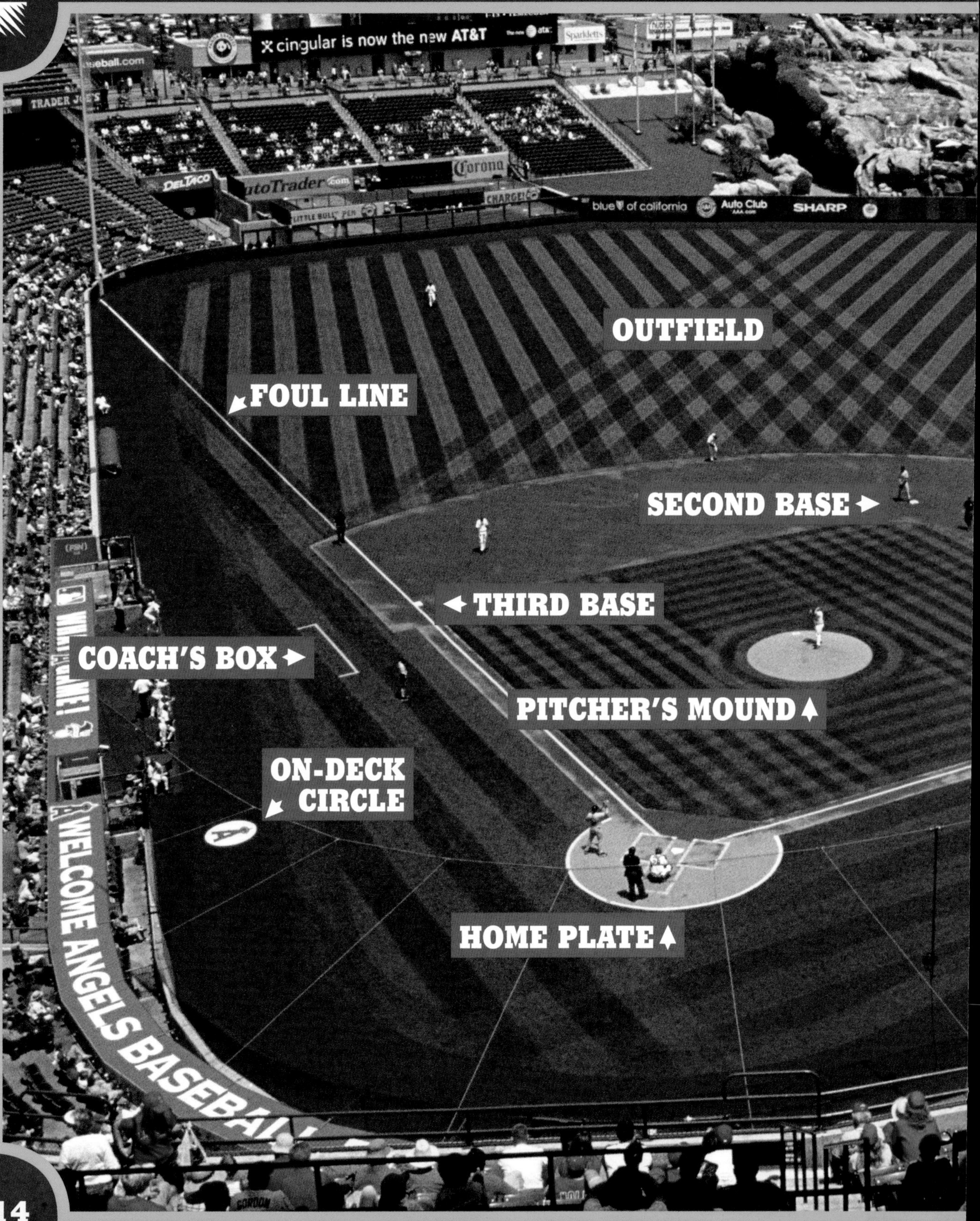

OUTFIELD

FOUL LINE

SECOND BASE ▶

◀ THIRD BASE

COACH'S BOX ▶

PITCHER'S MOUND ▲

ON-DECK CIRCLE ↙

HOME PLATE ▲

THE BASEBALL FIELD

INFIELD
FOUL LINE
FIRST BASE
DUGOUT
TOSHIBA
WHAT A GAME!
BASEBALL '07

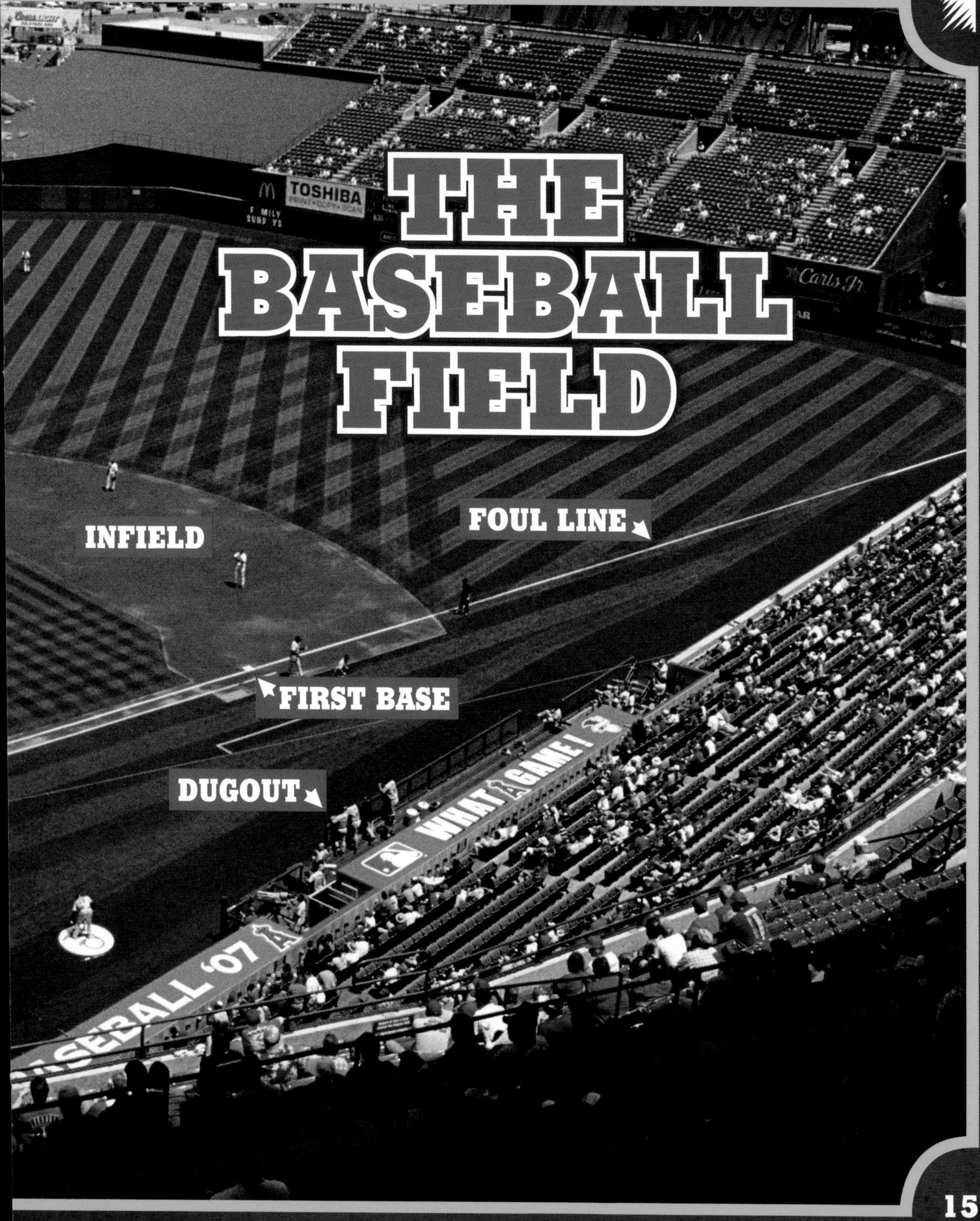

BIG DAYS

The Angels have been part of California baseball for more than 50 years. Here's a look at some of the most famous Angels events.

1973—Nolan Ryan was a superstar pitcher, one of the best of all time. In 1973, he threw two **no-hitters** for the Angels! In May, he beat the Kansas City Royals, only allowing three walks. Then two months later, he struck out 17 Detroit Tigers. It was his second no-hitter of the season.

Angels players celebrated after winning the 2002 World Series. ➤

1979—The Angels made it to the **postseason** for the first time. However, they lost to the Baltimore Orioles in the **ALCS**.

2002—The Angels made the playoffs as a **wild card**. In the playoffs, they **upset** the New York Yankees. The Angels then beat the Minnesota Twins in the ALCS. In the Angels' first-ever World Series, they beat the San Francisco Giants in seven games!

TOUGH DAYS

Every season can't end with a title. Here's a look back at some games and seasons Angels fans might want to forget!

1980—This was a tough season. The previous year, the Angels had made it to the ALCS. They fell hard in 1980. Their 65–95 record was the worst in team history. They finished 31 games behind the first-place team.

1986—In the 1986 ALCS, the Angels got off to a good start. They were ahead of the Boston Red Sox, three games to one. Then Boston won Game 5 in 11 innings. In Games 6 and 7, the Angels allowed 18 runs. They lost both games and the series.

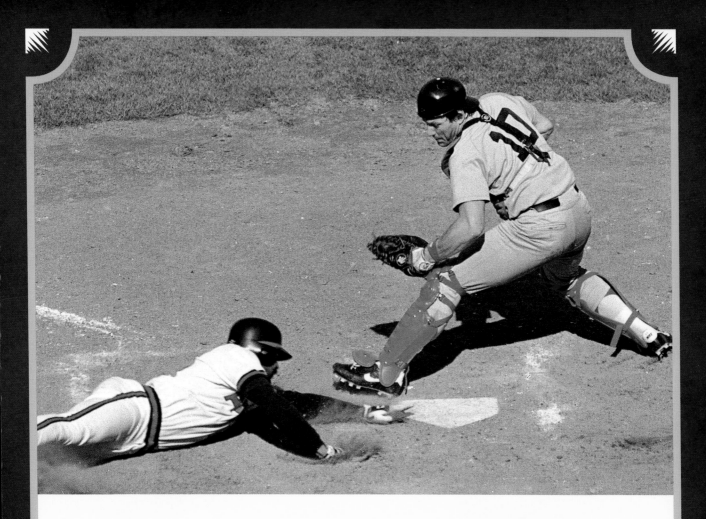

▲ *Ruppert Jones was safe here, but the Angels lost to Boston in 1986.*

2004 through 2009—The Angels were pretty good in these seasons. They made the playoffs five times. However, they flopped in the postseason. Beginning in 2004, they went on a nine-game playoff losing streak.

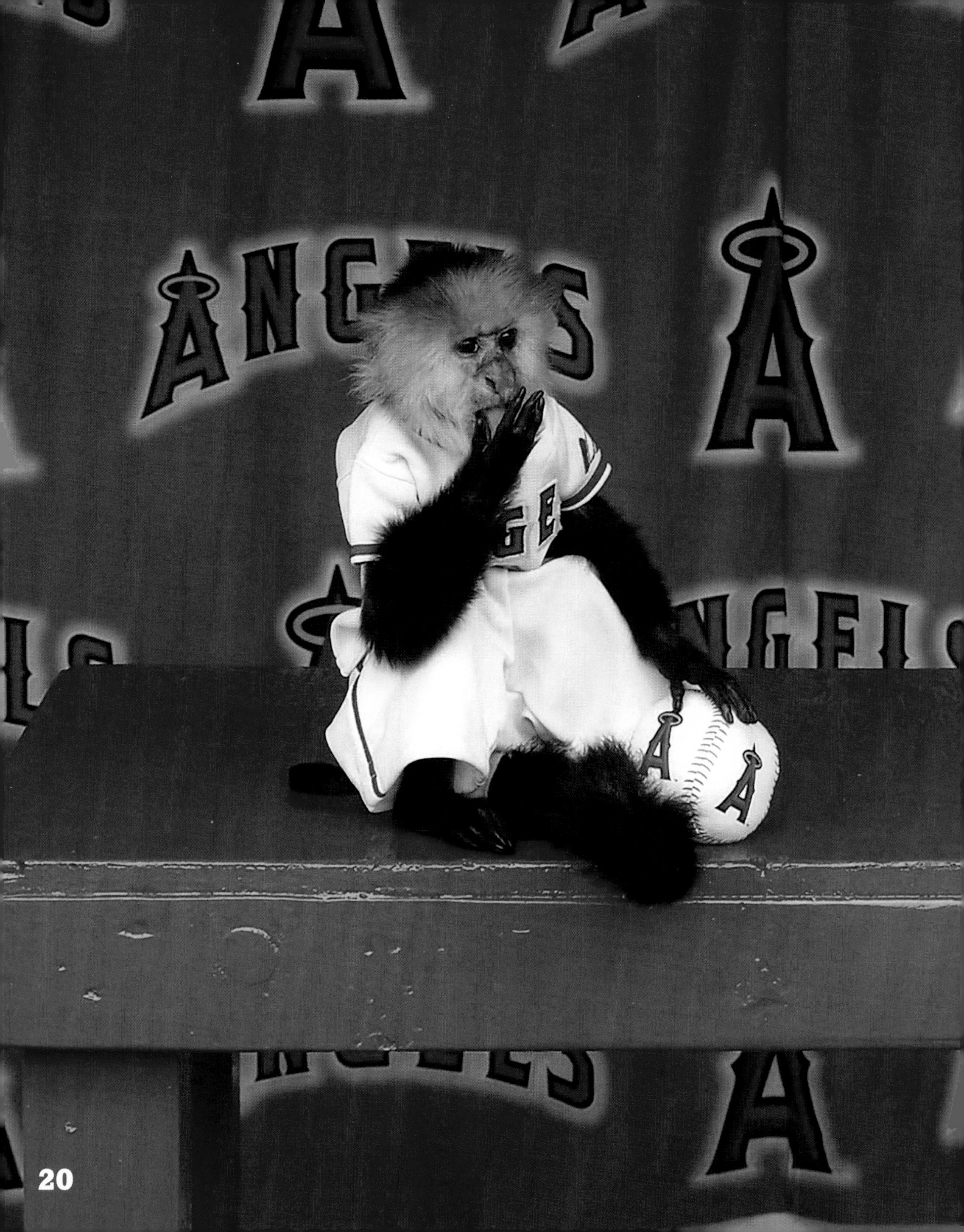

MEET THE FANS!

The Rally Monkey has been fueling Angels **comebacks** since 2000. He first showed up on the Angel Stadium video screen. Fans watched him flip and jump. They cheered . . . and the Angels won! So the Angels hired a real-life Rally Monkey. The fuzzy dude helped rally them to victory in Game 6 of the 2002 World Series. The Angels trailed by five runs but won the game! The Rally Monkey is still a big part of Angels games.

◄ *After a video monkey helped the team win in 2002, the Angels brought in a real monkey as a mascot.*

HEROES THEN

Nolan Ryan was the first Angels player to be inducted into the Baseball Hall of Fame. This power pitcher had an MLB-record 5,714 strikeouts. Vladimir Guerrero was a power-hitting right fielder. In 2004, he was the AL **MVP**. Guerrero joined Ryan in the Hall of Fame in 2018. Outfielder Tim Salmon was nicknamed Mr. Angel. Salmon played his whole 14-year career for the Angels. He was the AL **Rookie** of the Year in 1993.

Vladimir Guerrero had 173 homers in six seasons with the Angels. ➤

HEROES NOW

The Angels boast a powerful offense. Three hitters do most of the damage. Outfielder Mike Trout is probably baseball's best player. He was the 2012 Rookie of the Year. He has won two MVP awards. He has been an All-Star every full season he has played. Power hitting first baseman Albert Pujols is in the top 10 all-time for home runs. The Angels' newest star is Shohei Ohtani. He is from Japan. He is a great hitter and a great pitcher. Ohtani is one of the only players to do both of those things well.

◀ *Two-for-one: Shohei Ohtani is a great pitcher AND a top hitter!*

GEARING UP

Baseball players wear team uniforms. On defense, they wear leather gloves to catch the ball. As batters, they wear hard helmets. This protects them from pitches. Batters hit the ball with long wood bats. Each player chooses his own size of bat. Catchers have the toughest job. They wear a lot of protection.

THE BASEBALL

The outside of the Major League baseball is made from cow leather. Two leather pieces shaped like 8s are stitched together. There are 108 stitches of red thread. These stitches help players grip the ball. Inside, the ball has a small center of cork and rubber. Hundreds of feet of yarn are tightly wound around this center.

CATCHER'S MASK AND HELMET

WRIST BANDS

CATCHER'S MITT

CHEST PROTECTOR

SHIN GUARDS

CATCHER'S GEAR

TEAM STATS

H ere are some of the all-time career records for the Los Angeles Angels. All of these stats are through the 2018 regular season.

HOME RUNS

Tim Salmon	299
Garret Anderson	272

RBI

Garret Anderson	1,292
Tim Salmon	1,016

BATTING AVERAGE

Vladimir Guerrero	.319
Rod Carew	.314

STOLEN BASES

Chone Figgins	280
Mike Trout	189

WINS

Chuck Finley	165
Jered Weaver	150

SAVES

Troy Percival	316
Francisco Rodriguez	208

Nolan Ryan set a record with 383 strikeouts in 1973 for the Angels. ➤

STRIKEOUTS

Nolan Ryan	2,416
Chuck Finley	2,151

GLOSSARY

ALCS American League Championship Series, the playoff that determines the AL champion

comebacks (KUM-baks) when a team wins after trailing

minor league (MY-ner LEEG) a pro baseball group at a level below the Major Leagues

MVP Most Valuable Player, an award given to the top player in each league

no-hitters (noh-HIT-erz) games in which the starting pitcher or pitchers do not allow a single hit while winning the game

postseason (post-SEE-zun) the time after the regular season

rivals (RYE-vuls) two people or groups competing for the same thing

rookie (RUH-kee) a pro player in his or her first season

upset (UP-set) to win a game you are expected to lose

wild card (WYLD KARD) a team that makes the playoffs even if it doesn't win its division

FIND OUT MORE

IN THE LIBRARY

Machajewski, Sarah. *Mike Trout (Young Sports Greats.* New York, NY: PowerKids Press, 2018.

Morreale, Marie. *Mike Trout (Real Bios).* New York, NY: Scholastic Library, 2016.

Williams, Doug. *12 Reasons to Love the Los Angeles Angels.* Mankato, MN: 12-Story Press, 2016.

ON THE WEB

Visit our website for links about the Los Angeles Angels: **childsworld.com/links**

Note to Parents, Teachers, and Librarians: We routinely verify our web links to make sure they are safe and active sites. So encourage your readers to check them out!

INDEX